A Journey throughout time:

a collection of poems

Melissa Sherry

BALBOA.PRESS
A DIVISION OF HAY HOUSE

Balboa Press books may be ordered through booksellers or by contacting:

Balboa Press
A Division of Hay House
1663 Liberty Drive
Bloomington, IN 47403
www.balboapress.com
844-682-1282

ISBN: 978-1-9822-6294-5 (sc)
ISBN: 978-1-9822-6295-2 (e)

Print information available on the last page.

Balboa Press rev. date: 01/28/2021

A Fairy Kingdom Treasure

Though the air came a cry from the Lark, way on high
O'er the land of the Fairy Kingdom.
There was something amiss! Not to dismiss
Causing everyone there to go numb.

"Take Teed, take heed I beckon you
This news I have for you is true.
Someone so bad, someone unsee
Has stolen your beloved Fairy Queen."

The news not glad, all were sad
Who could do such horrible deed?
To play such a joke on such innocent folk
Of this they could not conceive.

The Fairies of the land did mourn
Of this I'm sure their hearts were torn.
For someone- who knew? Had gone astray
And stolen their beloved Queen away.

The search began both far and wide
Looking everywhere for who did hide.
And nothing, nil had yet to be found
Neither in the trees, nor on the ground.

They questioned all, both night and day
To see which "Someone" had gone astray.
But nothing amiss, nor clue to be found
Not one person to impound.

How sad they were to think her gone
And never more to be.
Their love locked away in their hearts to stay
For 'twas their Queen who held the key.

Now in the land of make believe
There lives both good and evil.
At times like this it's hard to miss
To divide it down the middle.

The flowers lost all their scent and color
The tress the leaves did shed.
The grass turned brown, weeds grew all around
It was like the land was dead.

"Who could do such a deed
Such a horrible deed?" Cried the Fairies throughout the land.
To play such a joke on such innocent folk
It has gotten quite out of hand.

All the birds in the air and the creatures below
Joined in search for their beloved Queen.
Looking here and there and everywhere
Still nothing had they seen.

The days became dark and the air grew cold
No food anywhere so I'm told.
The thought of her gone, what more could be said
Without her they all would be dead.

For she held the key, the magical key
That kept all of life there alive.
She had to be found, to be brought back
If not, they would not survive.

"Take heed, take heed, I beckon you"
Cried the Lark soaring above.
"I have good news about your beloved Queen
I do know she sends you her love."

"Oh please, oh please tell us so
Everything it is we need to know.
About our Queen and the horrible deed
So we can save here, of this we need."

So they gathered around to hear the news
And find out what they could do.
To find their Queen and save all life
To take their world out of its strife.

"It was the Ghouls of this I'm told
They though themselves brave and mighty bold.
To have stolen your Queen in such a way
Of this they will regret the day."

So all the Fairies far and wide
Came together, to decide.
The fate of those despicable fiends
To get back their Queen by whatever means.

Now the stypid Ghouls were not alone
Because by themselves, they had no backbone.
They needed the Gargoyles and a Troll
To steal the Queen, which was their goal.

So to find the enemies hiding place
The Fairies needed someone to interface.
To become one of them, to get inside
To find their Queen, that the fiends did hide.

The Oleander Fairy, bittersweet so they say
Stepped forward to help, to save the day.
Thought poisonous is he, he's full of charm
But for his Queen, he would do them harm.

The next to step forward to help in this plight
Was the Bindweed Fairy, who was ready to fight.
His strength in his stems, he creeps along the ground
Winding himself around all that he to be found.

The Laburnum and Greater Knapweed Fairies, too
Just tell them what they need to do.
They'd help save their Queen of this they would
They'd get her back and this was good.

The Fairies indeed needed not an army
To save their beloved Queen.
For the few that they had could be "Oh so bad"
And work together that they'd like a well-oiled machine.
For they saw that they had could be "Oh so Bad"

"Take heed, take heed oh villains do
For we are coming after you.
Our queen we'll save, no more to enslave
So know this you creatures your lives are grave."

So off they went to save their Queen
Going over the hills and through the ravine.
Straight to the place where she was kept
Unseen and quiet, so they crept.

The place they found was not so hard
A fortress high, but without a guard.
No one in sight with which to fight
But the dark was coming, so they'd wait til light.

The Bindweed Fairy, like his name
Crept up the walls a flame.
The other Fairies ascended the fortress high
To save their Queen, the enemy would die.

The Troll was on duty outside her door
Because he was big, who would need more?
But he was not smart and there he slept
So the Queens Fairies… in they crept.

They saw him asleep outside her door
Oh how lucky they were who could ask for more?
But careful they were so as not to awake.
He would alert the others, their Queen was at stake!

The Bindweed Fairy decided to creep by the door
And when the Troll awoke he'd be tied to the floor.
So he couldn't cry out or say any word
The Bindweed Fairy wound around, he wouldn't be heard.

Now the Oleander Fairy, bittersweet, so they say,
Entered the Queen's room, today was the day.
Take her back to her kingdom, that was the goal
And captures the enemy, tie them up like the Troll.

The Queen was inside ready to go
She knew they would come, still she was very low.
The harm that was done to her Kingdom below
The enemy would pay, for this she did know.

Quiet as mice not a word they spoke
Silence was necessary, this was no joke.
They needed to leave, steal away ere night
Before her Kingdom was lost, she must reunite.

The Troll was tied up, asleep at his post
So they crept slowly passed him just like a ghost.
Their silence important so he would not wake
To alert the others would be his mistake.

The Laburnum Fairy escaped with the Queen
They fled down the vine to wait in the ravine.
Where the others would meet after their score
They would capture the enemy, who would harm no more.

With the Queen Safely gone, and a job to complete
All the Fairies united the enemies to defeat.
A Troll all tied up unable to alarm
The Gargoyles on duty a cinch to diarm.

The Knapweed Fairy so strong and so true
Would capture the Gargoyles, she knew what to do.
For she had within her a scent that was sweet
They'd think she was harmless, of them she'd defeat.

As she approached the Gargoyles they took a stance
She emitted her scent, put them into a trance.
They dropped like flies, on the floor they laid
Asleep for now, that was how they stayed.

The next to find were the rotten Ghouls
It wouldn't be easy to find those fools.
For they hide in places not easy to see
But the Fairies would find them, I guarantee.

"Take heed, take heed oh villains do
For we are coming after you.
So hide you Ghouls," cried the Lark.
"We'll find you even in the dark."

The search went on long into the night
But still the Ghouls stayed far out of sight.
Until one fool thought no one was there
The Fairies were alerted and so set the snare.

As the Ghouls came out into the light
They were met by the Fairies, ready to fight.
The Ghouls tried to escape back through the door
They were snared by the Bindweed Fairy upon the floor.

Then all were caught and rounded up
Ready to transport—without mix up.
They'd take their captives to the ravine
And there they would meet up again with their Queen.

Their Queen arrived with the captives in tow
Indeed she was alive don't you know
The crowd shouted out with wild glee.
Now their lives would really be free.

The trial began swiftly without any wait
Now the enemy stood all alone.
No one would help them or participate
The enemy need to atone.

All silence fell still upon the court
The prisoners were then made to rise.
As the verdict was read, they knew that was said
For their crime had indeed… not been wise.

The sentence was passed, it was over at last
The prisoners were dragged from the room.
Their lives were not spared, they were not prepared
For what the Queen had awaiting their doom.

Now the Ghouls cried their innocence
The Gargoyles did the same.
Instead they pointed to the Troll
And said he was to blame.

But the Queen knew whose fault it was
Who stole her from her Fairy land.
And she would bring them all to trial
In front of the Kingdom they would stand.

"Take heed, take heed, I beckon you."
Cried the Lark soaring above.
"Your Queen is saved, now coming home.
The enemy is caught and she sends her love."

The cheer that went up both far and wide
Could be heard throughout the land.
The grass turned green, the trees came alive
Life did return to the Fairyland.

They begged and pleaded, their lives to be spared
But fell on deaf ears. They were made to be scared.
For kidnapping the Queen was the worse crime indeed
So their demise would be quick, accomplished with speed.

As night time fell on the Kingdom below
The moon above gave an ominous glow.
A last meal was given to the prisoners… they ate
Of the "Oleander cake". It was too late.

When morning arrived, 'twas a brand new day
The Kingdom came alive in a special way.
In the air was a song with a sweetness below
And all over this land was a wonderful glow.

"Take heed, take heed", cried the Lark soaring above.
"I've come with news of peace and of love.
Come gather around your Queen today
Life is once again safe in the Kingdom," I say.

The End
By: Melissa Sherry 2003
This took 4 years to write.

"This Garden Of Yours"

Lillies and Roses, Hydranges and Phlox,
Can all grow together in a big planter box.
With Marigolds and Asters and Allisums too,
A few springs of heather and a wandering jew.

A carpet of moss rose, a hint of comlumbine,
Make a delicate setting for butterflies to dine.
A Hummingbird's treat in this garden of yours,
Is the sweet taste of Verbena, this he adores.

A little fat bee at just the right hour,
Flies down to collect gold from every last flower.
He carries this necture on legs very strong,
Mixing the pollen as he goes along.

With faces held high, on very strong stems,
They denote a rich treasure these bright little gems.
He makes sure to pollinate all the flowers that day,
Then carries his treasure to a hive far away.

With the sun high above shining down on the ground,
War,ing the soil for when night comes around.
Then the flowers bow their heads, completing their chores
And fall fast asleep in this garden of yours.

With the dawning of day the sun does arrive,
Warming the flowers they all come alive.
Then come one and all to repeat all their chores,
To complete the cycle in this garden of yours.

By: Melissa Sherry.
July 16, 1996.

Magic in the night

As night time does descend
Upon the Garden wall.
It brings a bit of magic,
It beckons one and all.

To come, sit and listen,
A concert or play perchance?
With an impish elf and brownie,
And fairies in a dance.

The stars above will twinkle,
And the moon shine down it's beam.
It will brighten up the stage below,
Like magic, perchance a dream.

The notes of music that you hear.
Come from the lily pad.
Frogs play for you a joyful tune,
One that's sure to make you glad.

A note of two from crickets
As they rub their legs together.
Are music to your ears I'm sure,
Of this you will concur.

Your interest this I know will peek.
While sitting in a trance.
That's created by the elves and brownies,
And the fairies in their dance.

When nighttime slowly wanes from view,
And the concert is complete.
The magic is not lost, you'll see
It becomes a nightly treat.

BY: Melissa Sherry
7/26/96.

"After the rain"

Life goes on even after the rain,
The clouds have disappeared, life is whole again.
The storm is no more, it is gone this day,
The sun's shining bright, may the clouds stay away.

Everything is fresh and clean so it seems,
There is magic in the air, this is not a dream.
The birds are all singing and the flowers in bloom,
There is joy in my heart instead of gloom.

Life goes on even after the rain,
It brings a wanting to start again.
To make things new and to become a part,
Of a wonderful life with a brand new start.

BY: Melissa Sherry
July 21, 1996.

"Sweet Peas"

Early in the morning
While wearing drops of dew,
You hold your perky head up high
And sunbeams shine on you.

Sometimes I think you're naughty,
Saucy and a little shy,
And yet you bow with modesty
To all the passers-by.

I'm wondering at the close of day
If you whisper sweet love sonnets,
And while I look the other way
Steal kisses beneath your bonnets.

BY: Melissa Sherry.
July 26, 1996.

"Looking Back"

If I could see me standing
Back where I used to be,
I'd see a glimpse of someone else
Not who today I see.

I'd see a small undaunted child
Whose love and trust carefree,
Instead I find that I've become
The person that I see.

I'd see a small undaunted child
Whose love and trust carefree,
Instead I find that I've become
The person that I see.

I love but for a moment
And trust not one for me,
I fear for peace and happiness
I'm tossed upon the raging sea.

If I could see me standing
Back where I used to be,
I'd want to become that someone else
Not who today I see.

By: Melissa Sherry
July 26, 1996.

"Scarecrow"

Out in the field among the furrowed rows,
In the middle of the garden where the sweet corn grows.
With his arms outstretched and his head bowed low,
He's the sentry on duty, he's the lonely scarecrow.

He guards the corn that grows so tall,
And flaps at intruders big or small.
The stance he has is one of pride,
Of self-respect one feels deep inside.

From dusk till dawn he does his job,
The corn is safe, both kernel and cob.
The birds fly above and wait their chance.
To swoop down on the field, to make their advance.

He hangs on the pole pretending to be asleep,
With his head bowed low not making a peep.
He waits for the creatures both above and below,
And when they arrive, he gives them the heave-ho.

They'll not return the rest of the day.
They'll leave the field, they'll stay away.
He'll remain on duty because it's his job,
And guard the corn, every last cob.

By: Melissa Sherry 1995.

"Swallows"

When God made the swallows,
He gave it lots of thought.
And when he was finished,
They learned all that he taught.

For when they soar high up in the air,
Their grace and speed is beyond compare.
The games they play of dive and chase,
Leave patterns on your mind of delicate lace.

They weave in and out,
Passing ever so near.
Without worry of collision,
Without doubt or fear.

They are busy indeed,
When it is the time.
For the building of nests,
Is done with rhythm and rhyme.

They are busy indeed,
With the tasks ahead.
With the gathering of mud,
For the baby birds bed.

When work is completed,
And all are at rest.
God looks down with a smile,
And knows they did their very best.

BY Melissa Sherry 1995.

Melissa's Poetry corner:

"Heaven and Earth"

There's a beginning and an ending to life so I'm told,
One minute you are young, the next you are old.
And all of life that comes in between,
Is either wonderful and good or a sight not seen.

With all we are given and all that we learn,
We should feel quite safe, no room for concern.
But life's not that easy, life's not that way,
Take one step at a time and live day by day.

And when it is time for your life to end.
God checks his list and finds you did not bend.
The rules that he gave you, the lessons he taught,
Your love for him could not be bought.

Instead you withstood all temptations and shame,
And if you were wrong you took all the blame.
You never once hated or hurt out of spite,
You followed his teachings, afraid of his might.

And when that time for you is here,
You'll go to him gladly, without any fear.
Be ready and willing for that blessed event,
We'll be sad that you've gone, you'll be happy you went.

Life in heaven is majestic, more wonderful than here,
No more strife, no more hate, not even a tear.
And all come together, all love does abound,
For there's no greater place in this world to be found.

By: Melissa Sherry 1995.

"My little Chickadee"

With that little black cap upon your head,
And your grey tuxedo and tails.
With your creamy vest and black pant legs,
You're a sight to see, indeed well-bred.

You're a perky little creature, with a wonderful name.
You are honest and trustworthy, humble and tame.
You are respectful of others and dominate none,
You like to frolick and play and just have fun.

When you soar in the air and fly up to a cloud,
Your aerial acrobats indeed make you proud.
You are tiny but tough and fast as can be,
Always friendly and cheerful and very carefree.

When you fly in for a meal or just a treat,
You do somersaults first, then land on your feet.
You entertain when you can and offend not a one.
For pleasing others is just what is done.

When I outstretch my hand, I welcome you come,
To partake of the treat even if just a crumb.
You land with a lightness, a feathery touch,
It's not hard to remember why I love you so much.

When summer is gone and winter is here,
You never abandon me, you are always near.
To cheer me up when winter is long,
And sing to me your CHICK-A-DEE-DEE song.

So my proud little bird with tuxedo and tail,
I'll keep your feeders full, I will not fail.
Come visit me soon and stay for a while,
I need your friendliness, I need your smile.

BY: Melissa Sherry 1995

"The Hunter"

It was early one morning, the sun was just right,
Not a creature was stirring, nothing was in sight.
That cat, she lay basking in the sunlight so bright.
She'd roll and she'd stretch with all her might.
The sky was clear, there was dew on the ground.
The air was clean and still, there was not a sound.
She lay there quite regal, looking all around.
She was surveying her kingdom, seeing what could be found.
The sun was rising higher, still no breeze in the air,
It was getting hotter and putting a shine to her hair.
When all of a sudden a noise she did hear,
It was coming from somewhere, somewhere quite near.
She listened very closely, not a sound did she make,
She readied her body for the position she would take.
The sound that it made was something she had never heard,
So she lay there quite motionless, not uttering a word,
It was getting closer and soon it would be,
In range of her eyesigh and then she would see.
With her body poised and her muscles taut.
She was making ready for the pray that she saught.
The noise that she heard was as strange as could be,
She couldn't imagine what it was she would see.
She lay there with emotions all mixed up indeed,
Not knowing whether to run and hide, or stay and take heed.
When out of nowhere the thing did appear,
Yet not in front of her, but instead in the rear.
She froze in silence, her eyes getting big,
As she listened real carefully to the snap of the twig.
She turned with abound, her heart in her throat,
She was ready to pounce on the sound of a note.
When what to her wondering eyes should there be,
But the biggest bird that she ever did see.
It's legs were long, it's body large and in tact,
With the biggest eyes and lashes and that is a fact.
Both cat and bird were startled and surprised,
Neither could move, they were both mesmerized.

The local zoo had announced a bird got away,
And for everyone to look out for the Ostrich gone astray.
Well here they were, both scared and still,
Both wanted to moved but couldn't as if with no will.
The Ostrich was big and awkward as could be,
That's because it was a baby and that was plain to see.
The cat of coarse was at least a year old,
So that made a difference, it made her big, brave and bold.
Well nothing ever happened, they just sat and stared at each other,
Until the Zoo Keepers came and took the Ostrich home to it's mother.

BY: Melissa Sherry 1995.

"The Moon's afterglow"

As the fog slowly rises from the forest below,
And the moon casts it's light all around.
There are traces of something alive on the ground.
You can see shadows in the moon's afterglow.

There's a breeze in the air but it's not very much,
And the mist is so thick, it's damp to the touch.
The branches seem heavy and are hanging quite low,
They have an ominous look in the moon's afterglow.

There's an owl in the tree doing its nightly call,
There's the sweet sound of music from the close waterfall.
There's the smell of perfume from wild Jasmine that grow,
Near the base of the trees in the moon's afterglow.

There are frogs and crickets, who both sing a song,
And join together as a choir in a quaint sing-a-long.
There are bats with their wings that dive to and fro,
And dine on the bugs in the moon's afterglow.

A mouse scampers here and a moth flutters there,
They both seem too busy, they don't seem to care.
That something might get them, maybe they just don't know,
About the creatures that lurk in the moon's afterglow.

As night starts to leave and the moon slowly fades away,
It brings a promise of hope for the creatures of the day.
And rest comes to those who delight on the night, so
They can come out again in the moon's afterglow.

BY: Melissa Sherry 1995.

"Heroes in the Garden"

The lady of the garden
Is a small but powerful knight,
She lives among the leaves and stems,
Staying out of sight.

She works her way along the leaves,
Devouring as she goes,
Eating all the aphides
That are the plants mortal foes.

She flies from plant to plant
And is mighty so they say,
Some will try and catch her
But in flight she'll get away.

She comes in many colors
And in shades of red are true,
Sometimes a dot, a squiggly line
And maybe a stripe or two.

The other knight among the plants
Is straight and green and bold,
And if you're looking elsewhere
You'll miss it so I'm told.

It sits so very still
Upon a stem or leaf,
And snatches all the enemy
So quickly, it's almost disbelief.

At night time there are twinkling stars
That fly amongst the plants,
They bob around both high and low
Like fairies in a dance.

In daylight they do devour
All of the spider mites,
At night they eat the rest they miss
With the use of their glowing taillight.

BY: Melissa Sherry
July 26, 1996.

"My Special Place"

Once again in my garden, alone with my dreams,
I regain all my courage and self-esteem.
Here I patch up my heartaches and clean all my wounds,
Then I wrap myself up in a protective cocoon.

Where no harm can befall me, I'm safe as can be,
No one can enter here, in my garden I'm free.
The Sun always shines and the flowers smell sweet,
It is my safe haven, my place to retreat.

For when times are not good and people unkind,
It's a place that I go, to completely unwind.
I lose all my sadness, forget all my hurt,
I bury my troubles as I dig in the dirt.

My garden's not just for flowers, a carrot or beet,
It's a place that I go to that I can defeat.
All my problems and hurts and take away pain,
So I can emerge to start over again.

BY: Melissa Sherry
July 19, 1996.

The Rose

A rose is a flower with beauty abound
No other on earth could ever be found.
That equals the luster, the scent or the touch
God made it for all, for he loves us that much.
A rose is a gem with perfume divine,
No other is like it, it's one of a kind.
When God made the rose, it came from his heart,
So we could have love, right from the start.

Peace for all

There are stars in the heaves, they shine very bright,
Sometimes you can see them real late at night.
The skies will by cloudy, not a light can be seen,
Then the stars will appear, like the crown on a queen.
Their brightness shall shine for all to see,
So we can dream and pray for peace to be free.
There will come a time, when the stars will all shine bright,
Whether it is day or whether it is night.
The sky will open, and God will appear,
The light will shine bright, but without any fear.
All love shall abound and hatred shall cease,
For it is at that moment, that we shall have peace.

Dear God

Dear God give us strength and help us to love
All creatures on land and even above.
Help keep us safe from hard all around,
And show us the way to you to be found.
Our wanting of peace is still in our heart,
We sing of your praise, we have from the start.
Our love for you is real, and will not be lost,
We shall keep it with us to whatever cost.
So please hear our prayers, and keep us with you,
We need you dear God, in all that we do.
The road won't be easy, our steps not too kind,
Our days and our nights sometimes hard to find.
But with prayer on our side, our faith can withstand,
All trouble and strife, we're safe in your hand.

Friends

Friends are special, friends are kind
Some are bold and some are refined.
Some are brave and some are daring
Some are strong but never without caring.
Their love is real, it's given without favors
They like you no matter, they act like your savior.
They'll keep you from harm, no matter who's fault
They'll keep you safe and free from assault.
They'll tell you you're wrong, they'll tell you you're right
They'll stand by your side and put up a fight
They care without question and love with a might
They'll be your friend by day and by night.
They ask not a word, their love is for free
It's yours for the keeping, so please let it be.

"Violets & Pansy's"

Violets are for friendship and Pansys are for thought
They were put on this earth for us to be taught
The meaning of love, of caring and trust
The meaning of sharing and believing's a must.
They both go together, they go hand in hand
It's part of his Glory, it's part of His plan
He planted them both very close to the ground,
He gave them both colors, that could never be found
He gave them a beauty to be seen all around.
They give us a feeling, that's felt with abound.
Their fragrance is small, but never the less strong
If you keep them real close to you, you'll never go wrong.
That's why violets are for friendship and Pansys are for thought
They were put on this earth for us to be taught.

BY: Melissa Sherry
1998

"Whispers of memories"

Like the distant glow of ambers
From a fire built at noon,
They still shine bright in the dead of night
Those whispers of memories under the moon.

You can see them when you close your eyes
Or when you're wide awake,
They are with you just as plain as day
Those whispers of memories you cannot mistake.

When thinking of the past and dreaming
Of how it used to be,
You'll conjure up a lovely repose
For those whispers of memories you see.

You'll keep them to you constant
And never let them out of sight,
But you can share them with the one you love
Those whispers of memories when the time is right.

BY: Melissa Sherry
Aug. 6, 1996.

"Life has a lesson"

Life has a lesson we all must learn,
Sometimes it's not fair, not even our turn.
We start without worry, not a care in the world,
The only to grow up and find we're unfurled.
Our lives have been tossed on a see all abound,
Our dreams have been lost, not to be found.
Like books without names just tossed on the shelves,
We know not of others, not even ourselves.
Our hearts grow heavy, and not without strife,
Our minds do go blank and our bodies without life.
And then on that day, that time in the season,
We all come together, he tells us the reason.
Why life has a lesson we all must learn,
We find that it is fair, and it is our turn.

BY: Melissa Sherry 1994.

Look at me now

I was once a rich man, with wealth untold,
I needed nothing, I could buy all I could hold.
Acquaintances of many I did attract,
But look at me now, all of these I do lack.

I lost my wealth in one fell swoop,
No longer standing straight, but now with a stoop.
My voice lacks laughter, my eyes are sad,
I've lost the positiveness that I once had.

I'm out on the street, it's damp and cold,
I'm neither brave, nor am I bold.
I watch my back from all evil around,
I hide at night, so as not to be found.

As in my lonely time I spend thinking,
My thoughts are sad, my heart is sinking,
Will I ever come back to where I had been,
Or remain with poverty and not even clean.

I feel deserted, afraid and dispare,
Like no one knows me or even cares.
If I could change things, I would try,
To make my life better and not want to die.

If only God had not deserted me,
Maybe things would be better and I'd feel free.
Instead of this lonely hollow shell,
I'd still be the man you knew so well.

But wait—I'm not alone for God is still there,
There's footsteps behind me, he really does care.
Through all that has happened, God never left me,
Now I know I'll be safe, with his love I'll be free.

BY: Melissa Sherry

"Us four"

As little children, A boy and three girls,
We were our parents' precious little pearls.
Always loved and cared for, never left alone,
Even today and we are all full grown.

Our troubles and spats amongst us four,
Are all forgotten, thrown out the door.
We've come at last the long way home,
To be a family, never more alone.

BY: Melissa Sherry
Aug. 19,1996.

"Love from the Heart"

Tis that time of season when things are grand,
When folks are happy, it's a wonderland.
The air is crisp, the leaves are falling,
There is music in the air and our hearts are calling.
For peace on earth and good will towards men,
For love to abound all around us and then.
We can share in the birth and give praise on high,
All glory to God and his Son who did die.
To save our souls and be free from sin,
Put God in your heart and give love from within.

Melissa Sherry

"Faceless Courage"

Courage is loving when loving's not there,
Courage is giving with more than just care.
For holding back anger and hatred with a sigh,
For telling the truth instead of a lie.

For wanting of peace in a hate torn world,
Where bullets fly wild and racial slurs are hurled.
Where color still matters above all that's right,
It indeed takes courage to stand up and not fight.

Courage doesn't mean you are mighty and strong,
Courage means that you know right from wrong.
To stand up to evil with truth on your side,
Courage is what it takes, so do it with pride.

Melissa Sherry 1996.

Mothers

A mother is loving
A mother is divine
A mother is caring
A mother is kind.
She cares for her family
Her love is sincere
I know that God made her
That's why she's so dear.

That special time.

Easter is a special time
For loving and for praying
A time to think of Jesus
And all that he is saying
He gave his life so we may live
So we could care and we would give
Our hearts and love His will be done
To bring peace on earth to everyone.

He is special.

Time and time again we show
How much we care, How much we know
That God is good and God is great
He teaches us love and not to hate
He gave his son so we should live
A life of peace and always give
Our hearts to everyone all around
Full of caring, trust and love abound.

Dear God

Dear God give us strength and help us to love
All creatures on land and even above.
Help keep us safe from harm all around
And show us the way to you to be found.
Our wanting of peace is still in our heart,
We sing of your praise, We have from the start.
Our love for you is real and will not be lost,
We shall keep it with us at whatever cost.
So please hear our prayers and keep us with you,
We need you dear God, In all that we do.
The road won't be easy, Our steps not too kind,
Our days and our nights sometimes hard to find.
But with prayer on our side, our faith can withstand,
All trouble and strife, We're safe in your hand.

"What have we done?"

Daylight has dawned and not a sound can be heard,
There are clouds in the sky, but nary a bird.
Is flying on high nor swooping below,
Not even an animal moving to and fro.

The air is quite still, it has an ominous feeling,
Raising the hair in your neck, it's not very appealing.
Will the sun ever shine, are the clouds keeping it away?
Is there rain on the horizon, or just a nothing day?

The leaves have all fallen, they are deep and there's much,
They are brown and dry and will shatter at a touch.
Some branches have broken, the trees are all dead,
The hillside looks eerie, The land full of dread.

I stare at what happened and think of the past,
I try and compare but there is no contrast.
The sun use to shine and the breeze had a ring,
Bringing animals out to graze and making birds sing.

The trees all had leaves and the grass it did grow,
And after it rained there would be a rainbow.
All plants would grow and flowers would bloom
What a wonderful place, no look of doom.

Whatever has happened I'm sure it's our fault,
It had to be us who created this assault.
We have destroyed what God gave us, bow our heads in shame,
It is lost to us forever and nothing, will be the same.

BY: Melissa Sherry 1995.

When Tomorrow Starts Without Me

When tomorrow starts without me, and I'm not there to see,
If the sun should rise and find your eyes all filled with tears for me.
I wish so much you wouldn't cry the way you did today,
While thinking of the many things we didn't get to say...

I know how much you love me. as much as I love you,
And each time you think of me I know you'll miss me too.
But when tomorrow starts without me, please try to understand,
That an angel came and called my name and took me by the hand,
And said my place was ready in heaven far above,
And that I'd have to leave behind all those I dearly love.

But as I turned to walk away, a tear fell from my eye,
For all of life, I'd always thought I didn't want to die.
I had so much to live for, and so much left to do,
It seemed almost impossible that I was leaving you.

I thought of all the yesterdays, the good ones and the bad,
I thought of all the love we shared and all the fun we had.
If I could relive yesterday, I thought just for awhile,
I'd say goodbye and kiss you and maybe see you smile.

But then I fully realized that this could never be,
For emptiness and memories would take the place of me.
And when I thought of worldly things that I'd miss come tomorrow,
I thought of you, and when I did my heart was filled with sorrow.

But when I walked through heaven's gates I felt so much at home,
When GOD looked down and smiled at me, from His great golden throne,
He said, "This is eternity and all I've promised you
Today your life on earth is past but here it starts anew.
I promise no tomorrows, but today will always last,
And since each day's the same day, there's no longing for the past."

Because you've been so faithful, so trusting and so true,
Though there were times you did some things you knew you shouldn't do.
But you have been forgiven, and now at last you're free,
So won't you take my hand and share your life with me.

So when tomorrow starts without me, don't think we're far apart,
For every time you think of me, I'm right here in your heart.

Written by:
Melissa Sherry
Dec. 14, 2014.

"This wondrous world"

From the stars in the heavens that shine from above,
God is ever so present, he sends down his love.
From the trees and the flowers there is beauty all around,
With the waters and the mountains, the earth does abound.
He is ever so present in our minds and our heart,
He's been there from the beginning, he was there from the start.
All we have to do is just look and see,
At the beauty around us, it's wondrous as can be.
From the breeze in the trees and the songs from the birds,
From the sounds of the waters, like music not words.
From the eagles that soar up high in the sky,
To the creatures on the ground with four legs who can't fly.
God is ever so present on their minds and their soul,
For he has created all creatures and thus made them whole.

BY: Melissa Sherry
Oct. 25, 1994.

"The Stranger among us."

He's not what he seems when first he appears,
He's wrapped up in ribbons and lace.
He's not magic at all just a pandora's box.
When opened will crash in your face.

He'll appear to you one way so you'll not suspect,
The creature that lies underneath.
He'll be loving and kind, generous and sweet,
Then when you're not looking, he'll bare his teeth.

He'll whisper sweet things long into the night,
And feed on your love and your trust.
He'll keep you off guard, you'll surrender yourself,
Then he'll blow you away like you're dust.

It's hard to recover from a heart that has broken,
Has been ripped and shredded apart.
Your emotions are bruised and the wounds go deep,
He leaves a taste in your mouth that's real tart.

When finality comes and you walk away,
He will make you think it's your fault.
He'll not spare you mind and be very unkind,
Show no care, it's the final assault.

BY: Melissa Sherry
Aug. 13, 1996

"My sadness."

Today I embrace the silence, the emptiness and the loneliness,
I am numb.
You were a kindred spirit to me.
We were one at times in mind and heart,
Our love for the quiet country morning
Our love of the quiet country night.
I have known you for but a short while,
Yet I have known and will love you forever.
The love you had for your Father was so strong and real,
He has but to remember and not be sad,
My memories of you will not fade, but will bring me joy,
Where there is sorrow.
Your death was for not but my God will guide you,
You are safe with him.
God will keep you from harm.
I know in my heart we will meet again,
Be safe and know we love you.
You are going home and the journey is not long,
The path is clear and the light is glowing.
Good-bye my dear Jeff, we love you.
Until we meet again, I will at least have my memories.

BY: Melissa Sherry
Feb. 16th 1993.

Printed in the United States
By Bookmasters